DEADLY AND INCREDIBLE ANIMALS
INCREDIBLE ANIMALS
TOP 10 Snakes

Jay Dale

A+

Smart Apple Media
P.O. Box 3263
Mankato, MN, 56002

First published in 2011 by
MACMILLAN EDUCATION AUSTRALIA PTY LTD
15–19 Claremont St, South Yarra, Australia 3141

Visit our web site at www.macmillan.com.au or go directly to
www.macmillanlibrary.com.au

Associated companies and representatives throughout the world.

Copyright text © Jay Dale 2011

Library of Congress Cataloging-in-Publication Data

Dale, Jay.
    Top ten snakes / Jay Dale.
        p. cm. — (Deadly and incredible animals)
    Includes index.
    Summary: "Gives general information on features of snakes and threats to
    them. Counts down the top ten most dangerous snakes using a deadliness
    scale"—Provided by publisher.
    ISBN 978-1-59920-412-3 (library binding)
    1. Poisonous snakes—Juvenile literature. I. Title.
    QL666.O6D346 2012
597.96'165—dc22

                                    2010050058

Publisher: Carmel Heron
Commissioning Editor: Niki Horin
Managing Editor: Vanessa Lanaway
Proofreader: Georgina Garner
Designer: Cristina Neri, Canary Graphic Design
Page layout: Peter Shaw, Julie Thompson and Cristina Neri
Photo researcher: Legendimages
Illustrators: Andrew Craig and Nives Porcellato
Production Controller: Vanessa Johnson

Manufactured in China by Macmillan Production (Asia) Ltd.
Kwun Tong, Kowloon, Hong Kong
Supplier Code: CP February 2011

Acknowledgments
The author and publisher are grateful to the following for permission to reproduce copyright material:

Front cover photograph: Brown vine snake (Oxybelis aeneus) courtesy of Photolibrary/Jack Goldfarb.

Photographs courtesy of: ANTPhoto.com.au/John Cann, **5**, /Greg Fyfe, **27**, / Ken Griffiths, **13**, /Rob Valentic, **20**, /John Weigel, **29**; ardea.com/Mary Clay, **23**; AUSCAPE/Mike Gillam, **3**, **26**; Australian Red Cross, **30**; Thomas Calame, **25**; Corbis/Nigel J. Dennis/Gallo Images, **14**; Dreamstime.com/Amwu, **12**, back cover, /Benmm, **7** (bottom); iStockphoto/Andrea Zanchi, **4**; naturepl.com/Tony Phelps, **18**, back cover, /Robert Valentic, **22**, **28**; Photolibrary/Anthony Bannister, **6** (bottom), / David M Dennis, **24**, /Michael Dick, **11**, /Dinodia, **8**, /DV, **10**, /ER. DEGGINGER, **16**, / Paul Freed, **17**, /Michel Gunther/Mau, **19**, /Roland Symons, **15**; Pixmac/Fouroaks, **6** (top); Shutterstock/Susan Flashman, **21**, /markrhiggins, **9**, /Audrey Snider-Bell, **7** (top). Snake silhouette with 'That's incredible!' feature © Shutterstock/Paunovic, **7**, **9, 10, 12, 14, 16, 18, 20, 22, 24, 26, 28**.

While every care has been taken to trace and acknowledge copyright, the publisher tenders their apologies for any accidental infringement where copyright has proved untraceable. They would be pleased to come to a suitable arrangement with the rightful owner in each case.

The publisher would like to thank the Australian Red Cross for their help reviewing the first aid advice in this manuscript.

CONTENTS

GLOSSARY WORDS
When a word is printed in **bold**,
you can look up its meaning in
the Glossary on page 31.

DEADLY AND INCREDIBLE ANIMALS

Many animals are deadly to other animals. They are deadly to their prey and sometimes even to their **predators**. Over many thousands of years, these animals have developed incredible behaviors and features to find food, to defend themselves from predators, and to protect their young.

Deadly and Incredible Features and Behaviors

Different types of animals have different deadly features and behaviors. Deadly and incredible features include strong jaws, razor-sharp teeth, and stingers or fangs for injecting **venom** into prey. Deadly and incredible behaviors include stalking, hunting, and distracting prey before attacking and killing it.

Animals such as lions use their incredible size and strength to smash, crush and rip apart their prey. Excellent eyesight helps many **nocturnal** animals hunt their prey under the cover of even the darkest night.

A snake uses its venom to keep its prey still so it can swallow it whole.

DEADLY AND INCREDIBLE SNAKES

In deserts, forests, jungles, and even in your backyard, there live some of the world's most deadly and incredible snakes.

What Are Snakes?

Snakes are **vertebrates** that are part of a group called reptiles. They are scaly, cold-blooded animals that use their environment to warm their bodies. Land snakes can be found on every continent except Antarctica.

Venomous Snakes Around the World

There are about 725 different **species** of **venomous** snakes worldwide (including sea snakes). Venomous snakes are meat-eaters that hunt other animals. Their venom is used to keep their prey still so it can be swallowed whole.

IN THIS BOOK

In this book you will read about the top 10 deadliest land snakes on Earth — from number 10 (least deadly) to number 1 (most deadly). There are many different opinions on which snake should top this list. The snakes in this book have been selected on how poisonous their venom is, the amount that they inject, and how they attack their prey.

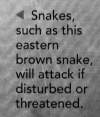

◀ Snakes, such as this eastern brown snake, will attack if disturbed or threatened.

FEATURES of VENOMOUS SNAKES

Venomous snakes have many features and behaviors in common. These deadly and incredible features and behaviors help snakes to survive in the environments in which they live.

Detecting Prey

Snakes have forked tongues that sense smells in the air or along the ground. The tongue passes in and out of the snake's mouth over a special part of the mouth called the Jacobson's organ, which helps the snake sense other animals.

▶ A snake uses its tongue to sense if there is an animal nearby, and to work out the animal's location.

Venom

All venomous snakes produce venom. Snake venom is poisonous saliva. It is produced in the saliva glands of venomous snakes. A snake uses its venom when hunting or in defense.

◀ A snake might use its venom when it is in danger. Some snakes can spit their venom when they are threatened.

Fangs

All venomous snakes have fangs to inject venom into their prey. Most snakes' fangs are fixed in the front of their mouths. Some snakes, such as vipers, have fangs that move. When these fangs are not in use, they fold back against the top of the snake's mouth. The fangs move forward when the snake opens its mouth and is ready to strike, or attack.

◄ Each of a snake's fangs has a tube-like hole through the middle, which allows the venom to pass through the fang and into the prey.

Flexible Jaw

A snake's jaw is incredibly flexible. It is made up of several sections, which can separate and allow the mouth to open extremely wide.

▼ A snake usually swallows its prey head first, so that it travels smoothly down the snake's throat.

That's Incredible!

Most experts believe the venom of the inland taipan is the deadliest of all land snakes' venom. Its venom contains enough poison to kill 100 healthy adult males. However, there have been no recorded human deaths from its bite.

THREATS to SNAKES

Over the past 300 million years, snakes have changed to become more suited to their environments, possibly more than any other species on Earth. Despite snakes' ability to adapt, most experts believe that the number of snakes worldwide is decreasing. This decline is due to the activities of humans.

Threats to Survival

Many snakes have become **extinct** and others are **endangered**. The Hoffstetter worm snake is extinct due to the introduction of predators into its **habitat**, which it was unable to protect itself from. The Alcatrazes lancehead (a viper) is considered critically endangered. This viper is found only on one small Brazilian island and its habitat is under threat.

There are currently 131 viper species listed on the International Union for Conservation of Nature Red List of Threatened Species. This means that these species could become endangered or extinct in the future. This is only one type of threatened snake.

◄ In eastern Asia, the king cobra is killed for meat and to make medicinal products. This threatens the species.

▲ A snake's venom is "milked" to make **antivenom**. Using snakes for medical research reduces their population, but helps to lower the number of human deaths from snakebite.

Habitat Loss

The biggest threat to snakes is habitat loss through logging and **deforestation**. When a snake's habitat is destroyed, so is the habitat of the prey it eats, which leaves the snake without enough food to survive.

Snake Trade

Many snake species are becoming endangered because people buy and sell them in the snake trade. Many snakes are illegally taken out of countries and sold as pets. Others are killed for their skin and meat.

Medical Research

Snakes are used in medical research to make antivenom. Snakes are not killed when antivenom is made, but they are held in cages. Snake skins, organs, and meat are sometimes used in other treatments, such as traditional Chinese medicine.

That's Incredible!

Around 250 types of venomous snakes have the ability to kill a human with one bite. Scientists have produced antivenoms for many of the world's deadliest snakes.

Introduced Predators

Animals that are introduced into a habitat, such as cats, dogs, and foxes, may prey upon snakes. As the number of introduced predators increases, the number of snakes decreases.

KING COBRA

When threatened or disturbed, the king cobra raises its head and one-third of its body, showing its "hood" and revealing its fangs. It often makes a loud, deep hissing sound as a warning.

▼ The king cobra's hood is made up of long ribs that extend to fill out the loose skin in the neck, behind its head.

That's Incredible!

Snake charmers that use king cobras are usually tattooed with ink that has been mixed with king cobra venom. Some say this protects them from being bitten.

wide, flat head

forked tongue

hood

smooth scales

long body

Deadly features: venom injected through fangs, which are up to 0.5 inch (1.25 cm) long

Predators: mongooses, humans

Size: average 11.8 to 13.1 feet (3.6–4 m) long; weight around 13 pounds (6 kg)

Lifespan: unknown

Habitat: tropical rain forest, also found near swamps and rivers

Distribution: ■
South and Southeast Asia, including parts of India, China, Vietnam, Malaysia, Indonesia, Thailand and the Philippines

Deadly Venom

The king cobra uses its deadly venom to **paralyze** and kill its prey. It holds on to its prey until the prey stops moving. It can produce large amounts of venom in one bite, and can bite more than once.

Killer Senses

The king cobra lowers its jaws to the ground to sense the movement and sounds of its prey. It uses a combination of this and its good eyesight to sense how far away the prey is.

What's for Dinner?

King cobras eat other snakes (mostly rat snakes), lizards, birds, rats, and mice.

▼ The king cobra has an incredibly strong bite and it hunts and eats other snakes.

DEATH ADDER

The death adder has the quickest strike of any snake in the world. In just 0.13 of a second, it can strike, inject venom into its prey, and return to its strike position.

That's Incredible!

Death adders can wait for prey, lying still and ready to strike, for many days.

short, tough body

triangle-shaped head

worm-like **lure** on the end of the tail

tail

vertical pupils

scales

▲ The death adder's short, muscular body allows it to strike at its prey quickly and powerfully from a still position.

Deadly features: fangs for injecting venom, speed of strike, camouflage

Predators: cats, foxes, humans

Size: up to 3.3 feet (1 m)

Lifespan: unknown

Habitat: open woodland and scrub

Distribution: ■
Australia and New Guinea

Luring Prey

The death adder has a lure on the end of its tail to attract prey. It wiggles its lure back and forth to make it look like a worm. When a bird or small animal grabs the "worm," the death adder strikes, killing its prey in less than a second.

Hidden Danger

The death adder is well camouflaged and can lie incredibly still. It uses its camouflage to hide in leaf litter and soil. Only its head and tail can be seen. It remains hidden during the day and starts hunting at dusk.

▼ The death adder strikes so quickly that the prey does not realize what has happened.

What's for Dinner?

Death adders eat small mammals and birds. They sometimes eat cane toads, which are poisonous and can kill the snake.

BOOMSLANG

The boomslang has folded fangs at the **rear** of its mouth, which unfold when the snake is ready to bite. It is the deadliest rear-fanged snake in the world.

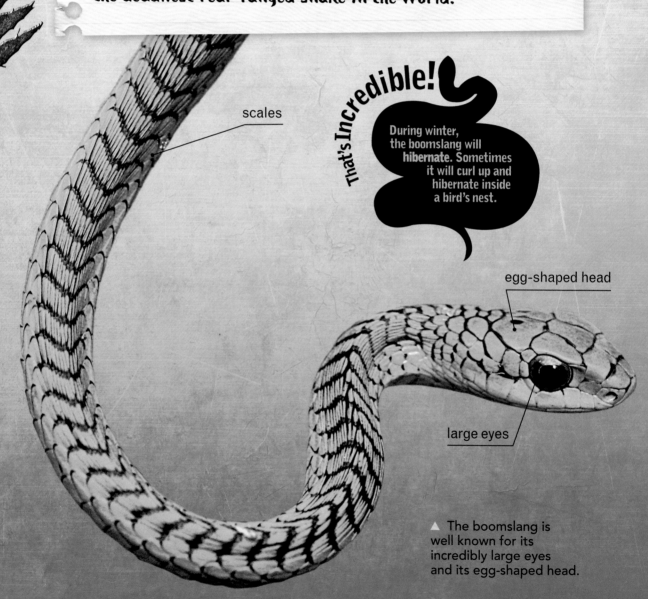

scales

That's Incredible!

During winter, the boomslang will **hibernate**. Sometimes it will curl up and hibernate inside a bird's nest.

egg-shaped head

large eyes

▲ The boomslang is well known for its incredibly large eyes and its egg-shaped head.

Deadly features: folded fangs for injecting venom, camouflage, quick movement

Predators: mongooses, honey badgers, feral or wild cats and dogs, humans

Size: 3.3 to 5.2 feet (1–1.6 m) long

Lifespan: unknown

Habitat: forests with trees and bushes

Distribution: ■
southern and sub-Saharan Africa

Tree Dweller

The word *boomslang* means "tree snake" in the Dutch and Afrikaans languages. The boomslang slides in and around branches in search of birds, birds' eggs, and lizards. When hunting, it waits among branches, often extending its body into an upright position. It can strike quickly, without warning.

What's for Dinner?
Boomslangs eat lizards, frogs, small mammals, birds, and eggs from nesting birds.

Deadly Dribble

The boomslang does not inject its venom through hollow fangs in the same way as other snakes. Instead, the boomslang's venom dribbles down its fangs and into the bite wound.

▼ The boomslang's coloring makes it well-camouflaged in the trees.

EASTERN CORAL SNAKE

The eastern coral snake is shy and spends most of its time underground or buried in leaves on the ground. It uses its colorful bands to confuse predators.

That's Incredible!

The eastern coral snake is related to the cobra snake. It has been seen lifting its head and part of its body off the ground as a warning, just like a cobra.

smooth scales

colorful bands

tail

black nose

head

▶ The coral snake is most active during early morning and evening, and is usually seen during the spring and fall.

Deadly features: fangs for injecting venom

Predators: eagles, hawks, mongooses, foxes, feral cats and dogs

Size: 20 to 30 inches (51–76 cm) long

Lifespan: unknown (up to 7 years in zoos)

Habitat: woody, sandy, and swampy areas

Distribution: ■ southeastern United States

Ambush Hunter

The eastern coral snake hides in a pile of leaves and **ambushes** its prey. It grabs the prey with its small fangs and chews it to inject the venom. Once the prey is paralyzed by the venom, it is slowly swallowed. The eastern coral snake then lies in the sun to warm up its body, to help digest the prey.

▶ After paralyzing its prey, the eastern coral snake starts to swallow it.

Colorful Killer

The eastern coral snake has striking colorful bands all along its body. It has thick bands of red and black with thin bands of yellow (or white), and a black nose. It confuses its predators by curling up into **coils** and lifting its tail as a "false head." When the predator grabs the tail — which it thinks is the head — the snake strikes back.

What's for Dinner?

Eastern coral snakes eat smaller snakes, lizards, frogs, nesting birds, and rodents.

17

SAW-SCALED VIPER

This small, **aggressive** snake will attack any creature or person that comes within striking distance. The saw-scaled viper has killed more people in Asia than all the other venomous snakes of Asia combined.

▼ The saw-scaled viper gets its name from the sound it makes when it rubs its side scales together.

That's Incredible!

The saw-scaled viper is also known as the "sidewinder" because of the way it travels over surfaces such as soft sand. It travels at a 45-degree angle to the line of its body.

serrated, **keeled scales** (on top)

short, round snout

scales that stick out (lower side)

Deadly features: fangs for injecting venom, aggressive nature

Predators: Egyptian cobra

Size: up to 26 inches (65 cm) long

Lifespan: unknown

Habitat: rural areas, fields, and dry, rocky areas

Distribution: ■
Africa, Asia and Middle East, including Sri Lanka, India, Pakistan, Syria, Iraq, Iran, Saudi Arabia, Jordan, Algeria, and Egypt

Sizzling Warning

The saw-scaled viper makes a sizzling warning sound when it is about to strike. It forms moving C-shaped coils with its body. This rubs its sides together and produces the sizzling sound, called stridulation (say *stry-dyoo-lay-shon*).

Strike and Swallow

The saw-scaled viper is an aggressive snake and is quick to strike. It kills prey by injecting poisonous venom into it, which causes **paralysis**. It then swallows the prey whole.

What's for Dinner?

Saw-scaled vipers eat locusts, beetles, worms, slugs, spiders, scorpions, centipedes, frogs, toads, other reptiles (including other snakes), mice, and birds.

As the saw-scaled viper gets angrier, it moves faster and the sound it makes becomes louder.

TIGER SNAKE

If threatened or disturbed, the tiger snake will flatten out its neck and raise its body off the ground in a frightening way. It may then make a sudden, loud hiss or barking sound as a warning.

▼ Tiger snakes range in color from jet black to yellow or orange, with grey or sandy bands. Some tiger snakes do not have any bands.

That's Incredible!

A female tiger snake may produce up to 125 live young during one breeding season.

fangs

scales

Deadly features: fangs for injecting venom

Predators: small-eyed snakes, birds of prey (including kookaburras), humans

Size: up to 6.9 feet (2.1 m) long

Lifespan: unknown

Habitat: coastal areas, woodlands, wetlands, and creeks

Distribution: ■ southern Australia, including Tasmania and coastal islands

▼ The tiger snake kills its prey by injecting its venom into the animal, and then swallows it whole.

Slow but Deadly

The tiger snake is a slow and careful hunter, but it is not aggressive. It enters the burrows of mice, rats, and rabbits to look for prey. It has been known to attack bird nests 26 feet (8 m) up a tree. It uses its fangs to inject venom into its prey before swallowing it whole.

Solar-powered Digestion

The black coloring of some tiger snakes allows them to warm up quickly in the sun. They need to warm up in the sun before they can go hunting. After a tiger snake has eaten a meal, it will lie in the sun. This helps the snake digest its prey.

What's for Dinner?

Tiger snakes eat small animals, such as mice, rabbits, birds, lizards, smaller snakes, frogs, and sometimes fish.

21

COASTAL TAIPAN

The coastal taipan is incredibly dangerous. It often strikes many times and very quickly if it is threatened. It injects more and more venom with every bite.

▼ The coastal taipan is a long, slender snake with a whip-like tail. It uses its tongue to sense prey.

scales

forked tongue

That's Incredible!

One coastal taipan has enough venom to kill up to 12,000 guinea pigs.

whip-like tail

Deadly features: fangs up to 0.5 inch (13 mm) long, for injecting venom

Predators: feral cats and dogs, humans

Size: up to 9.5 feet (2.9 m) long

Lifespan: unknown (7.5 years in zoos)

Habitat: coastal areas, including grassy beach dunes, dry and wet forests, and farmed areas such as cane fields

Distribution: ■
north and northeastern coastal areas of Australia

What's for Dinner?

Coastal taipans eat small mammals, including small rats, mice, bandicoots, and birds.

▶ The coastal taipan's venom is fast-acting, quickly paralyzing prey so that the taipan can start to eat it.

Strike and Release

The coastal taipan uses a "strike and release" hunting method. It lies incredibly still and then very quickly bites its prey and backs off. It waits for the venom to paralyze the prey before it starts to eat it. This hunting method prevents the prey fighting back with its sharp teeth and claws.

Warning Pose

When a coastal taipan is disturbed, it gives a deadly warning to frighten away any predators. It makes an S-shape and raises the front of its body off the ground. It moves the end of its tail very quickly from side to side.

MALAYAN KRAIT

The Malayan krait has a very small mouth and head compared to other venomous snakes. However, its venom is 16 times more deadly than a cobra's venom.

That's Incredible!

If a Malayan krait is exposed to sunlight it thrashes about. It tries to hide its head under its own body because it is desperate to find a dark place.

▼ The light and dark bands of color on a krait help to camouflage it at night, when it is active.

bands of light-and dark-colored scales

smooth, glossy scales

small head

Deadly features: fixed fangs for injecting venom
Predators: humans, feral cats and dogs
Size: up to 5.2 feet (1.6 m) long
Lifespan: unknown
Habitat: flat land close to water, particularly rice fields and rice dams

Distribution: ■
Sri Lanka, India, Pakistan, Bangladesh, Nepal, Bhutan, Cambodia, Vietnam, Burma (Myanmar), Malaysia, and Indonesia

Nocturnal Cannibal

The Malayan krait is a nocturnal hunter. During the day it stays hidden in the holes and nests of mice and rats. It is a cannibalistic snake, which means that it will eat other Malayan kraits. It has been known to enter people's homes at night when it is hunting for prey.

What's for Dinner?
Malayan kraits eat other snakes and lizards.

Paralyzing Venom

The venom of the Malayan krait causes paralysis. When it bites its prey, it holds on to it with its strong jaws until the victim is paralyzed.

▼ The Malayan krait hunts for reptiles at night. It sometimes enters people's gardens and homes looking for prey.

EASTERN BROWN SNAKE

The eastern brown snake is not always brown in color. It can be light brown, orange, or sometimes even black. It is often found living close to people's homes or in farm buildings, because its prey lives near people.

▼ The eastern brown snake has small, fixed fangs at the front of its mouth.

long, fast-moving body

small fangs

That's Incredible!

It can take several hours for the eastern brown snake to break down its prey. It may only need a few large meals a year.

scales

Deadly features: fixed fangs for injecting venom

Predators: feral cats and dogs, large birds of prey, humans

Size: up to 7.9 feet (2.4 m) long

Lifespan: 15 years in the wild (up to 26 years in zoos)

Habitat: open grassland, pastures, and woodland

Distribution: ■
eastern Australia, from the desert to the coast, and parts of Papua New Guinea and Indonesia

Powerful Poison

The venom of the eastern brown snake causes paralysis. This happens instantly in small prey. The eastern brown snake often has to hold on to larger victims with the coils of its body until the venom takes effect. It is an aggressive hunter that moves very quickly when chasing prey.

What's for Dinner?

Eastern brown snakes eat small mammals, such as mice and rats.

Defense Pose

The eastern brown snake takes on a defensive pose when it feels threatened. It raises its body off the ground, flattens its neck, and sways from side to side. It may bite its **predator** many times, injecting only a small amount of venom each time.

▼ The eastern brown snake sometimes coils its large, strong body around its prey until its venom takes effect.

INLAND TAIPAN

The inland taipan has the most powerful venom and is classed as the deadliest land snake on Earth. Even though there are no recorded human deaths from an inland taipan bite, one bite contains enough venom to kill 250,000 mice or 100 healthy men.

That's Incredible!

When there are large numbers of long-haired rats in the inland taipan's habitat, the taipan can become quite fat. The taipan loses weight when the rat numbers reduce.

▼ The inland taipan uses its fangs to inject its deadly venom.

small fixed fangs at the front

darker-colored head

scales

Deadly features: fixed fangs for injecting venom are 0.14 to 0.24 inch (3.5–6.2 mm) long

Predators: humans

Size: up to 8.9 feet (2.7 m) long

Lifespan: unknown (10 to 15 years in zoos)

Habitat: hot, dry areas

Distribution: ■
inland Australia

Cornering Prey

The inland taipan corners its prey in burrows or deep cracks in the soil. It then bites the prey quickly, sometimes several times. It normally uses the "strike and release" hunting method. Once it has bitten its prey, it follows the animal as it staggers away to die. It follows the animal's scent along the ground, and then eats it.

▼ The inland taipan hunts early in the morning or in the afternoon when the weather is cooler.

Shy Snake

Although it is also known as a fierce snake, the inland taipan is a shy snake. It usually slithers away from predators, such as humans. It will hide in leaf litter or gaps in rocks.

What's for Dinner?
Inland taipans eat animals such as the native Australian long-haired rat.

FIRST AID

Keep these first aid tips in mind if you or someone with you is bitten by a snake. Quick action can help minimize the impact of snake bites. You do not need to kill or capture the snake to identify it.

First Aid for Snake Bite

1 Keep the person calm, reassured, and still.
2 Apply firm pressure over the bite area. Use your hand if necessary.
3 Using firm pressure, apply a bandage over the bite area.
4 For a bite on the arm or leg, apply another bandage. Starting near the fingers or toes, firmly bandage upward, covering as much of the limb as possible. Keep the limb still by using a splint.
5 Seek medical help immediately.
6 Monitor the person and give CPR if needed.

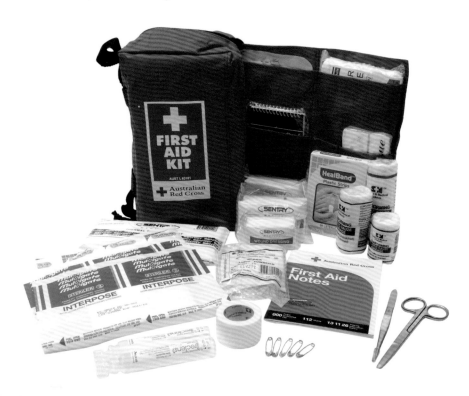

GLOSSARY

Aggressive Angry and often ready to attack

Ambushes Makes a surprise attack on

Antivenom Medicine that stops the effect of a poisonous sting or bite

Camouflage Spots, stripes, other patterns or colors on an animal that allow it to blend in with its environment

Coils Rings or loops

Deforestation The clearing of natural forests

Endangered In danger of becoming extinct

Extinct Wiped out, or no longer alive anywhere on Earth

Habitat The environment where animals and plants live

Hibernate Spend the winter at rest

Keeled scales Rough scales that have a ridge running down the middle

Lure A device, such as bait, used to attract prey

Nocturnal Active (usually hunting) at night

Paralyze Make the body unable to move

Paralysis Being unable to move

Predators Meat-eating animals that hunt, kill, and eat other animals

Rear The back

Species A group of animals or other living things that share similar features and behaviors

Venom A poisonous or harmful substance produced by an animal, which is injected by a bite or a sting

Venomous Containing harmful poison, called venom

Vertebrates Animals with backbones

INDEX

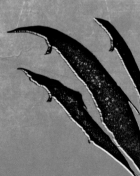